Christmas Moments
Bring Color to Your Christmas

Gayla McDonald

DEDICATION

I would like to dedicate this book to my husband, Will, and my son, Sean, for all of their support and understanding while I worked on this project. I would like to thank Dawn for being my cheerleader at work letting me know that I can do this. I would like to thank the children I help teach for their constant belief that, "I am an artist". Finally, a special thank you to my mother who taught me so much about what it is to express yourself through art.

Thank You All.

Gayla

I would like to invite you to sit down during this very busy time of year and pause. Pick up your colored pencils or pens and begin to ponder the wonders of Christmas. I hope that as your make your way through this book, page by page, you will think of those in your life that make this time of year special. Take a moment to think of the joy and peace that Christmas can bring and let that soak into your heart. While you bring sparkle and color to these pages, drink a cup of hot chocolate....yes, with marshmallows, or nibble on a candy cane.

May this year be full to the top with very special Christmas moments.

I am so glad that I can be a part of them.

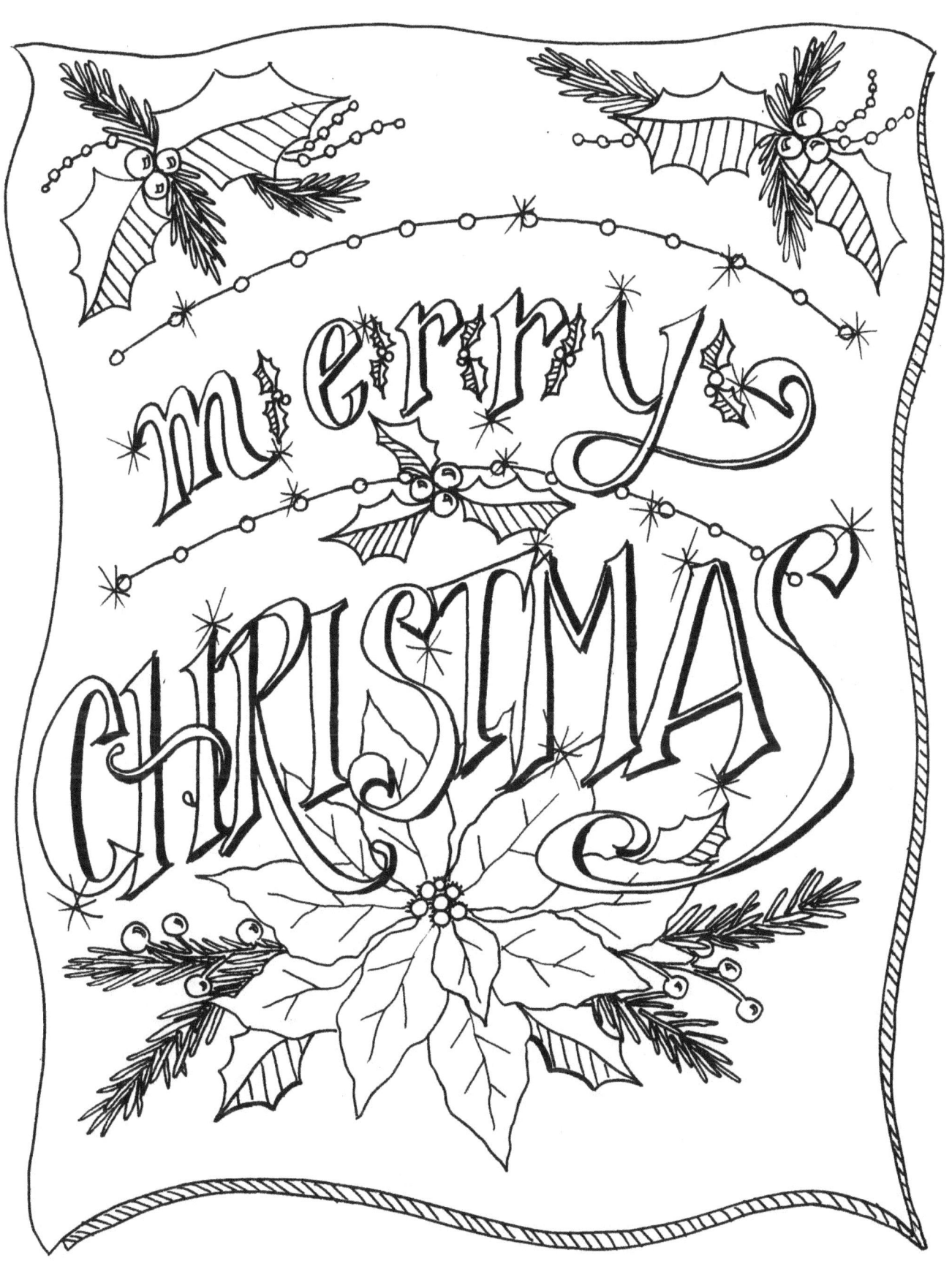

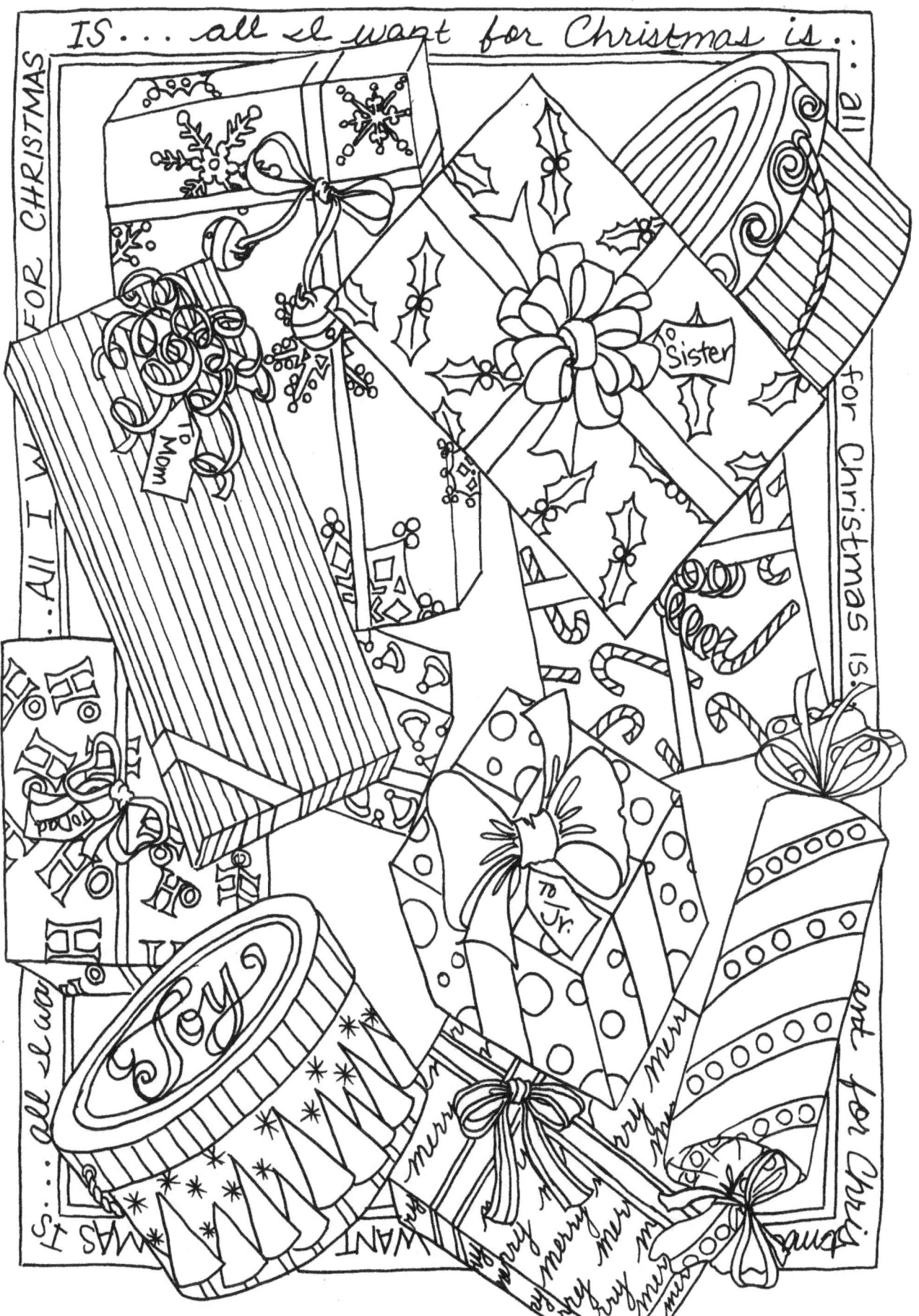

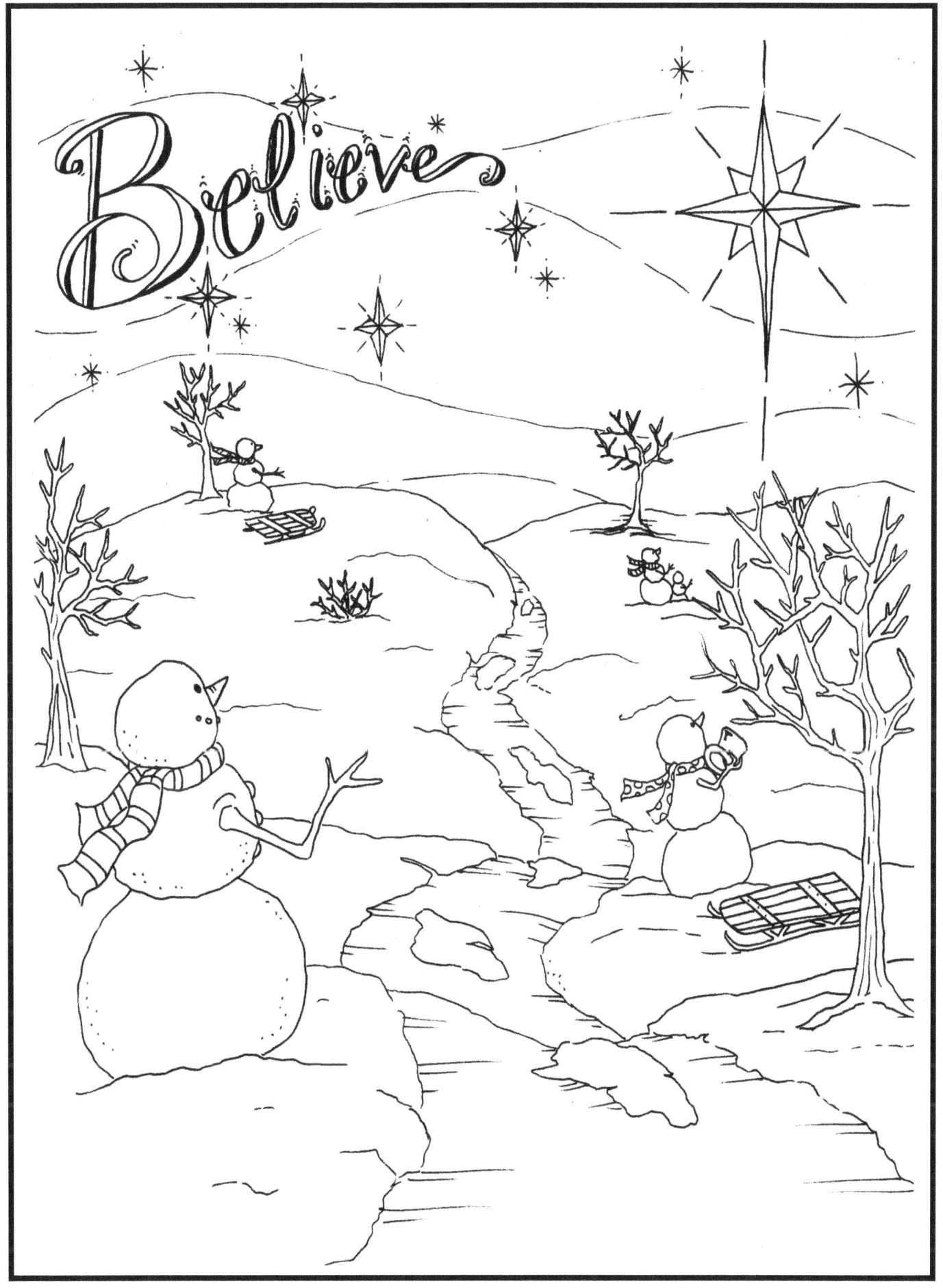

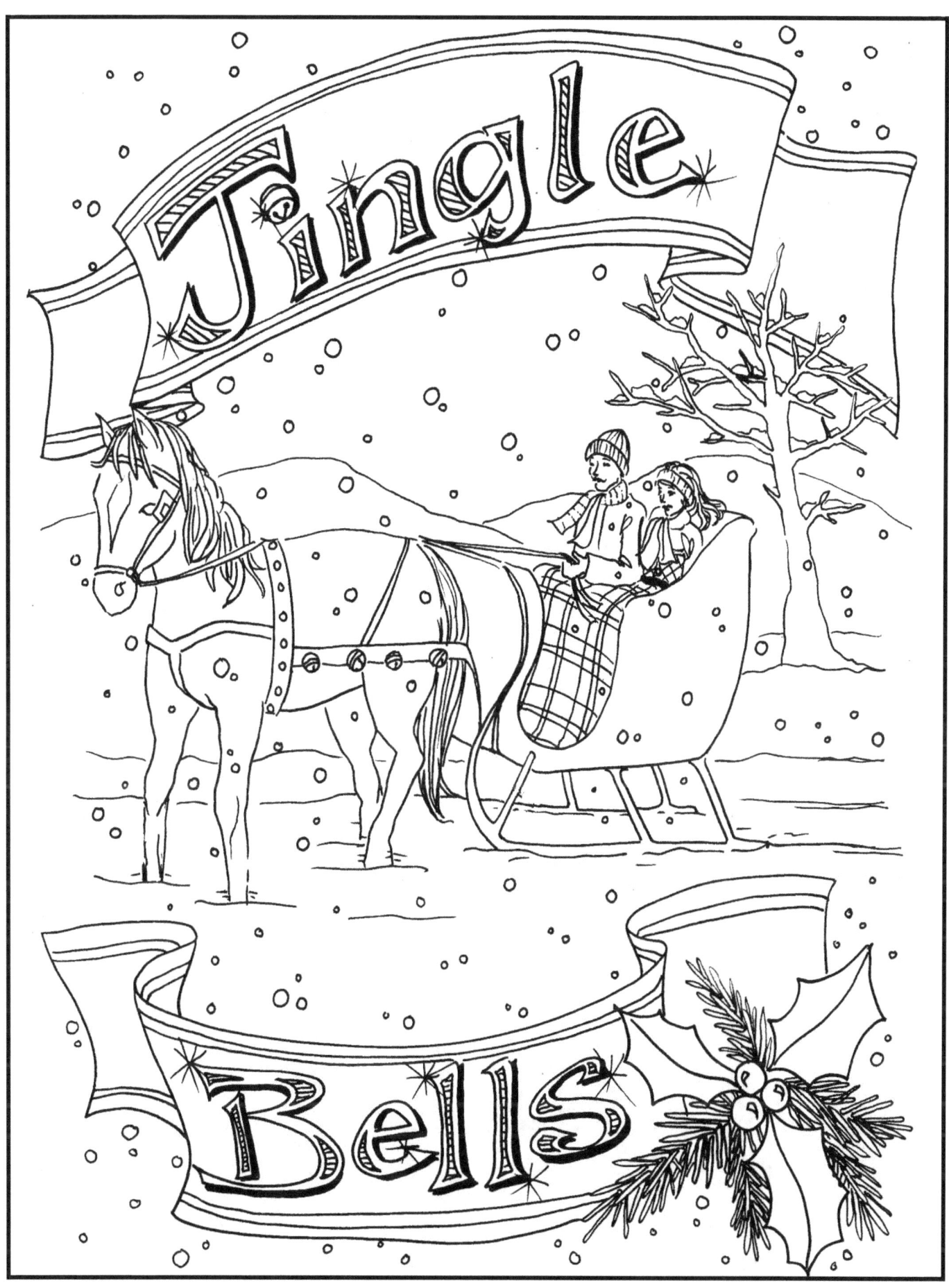

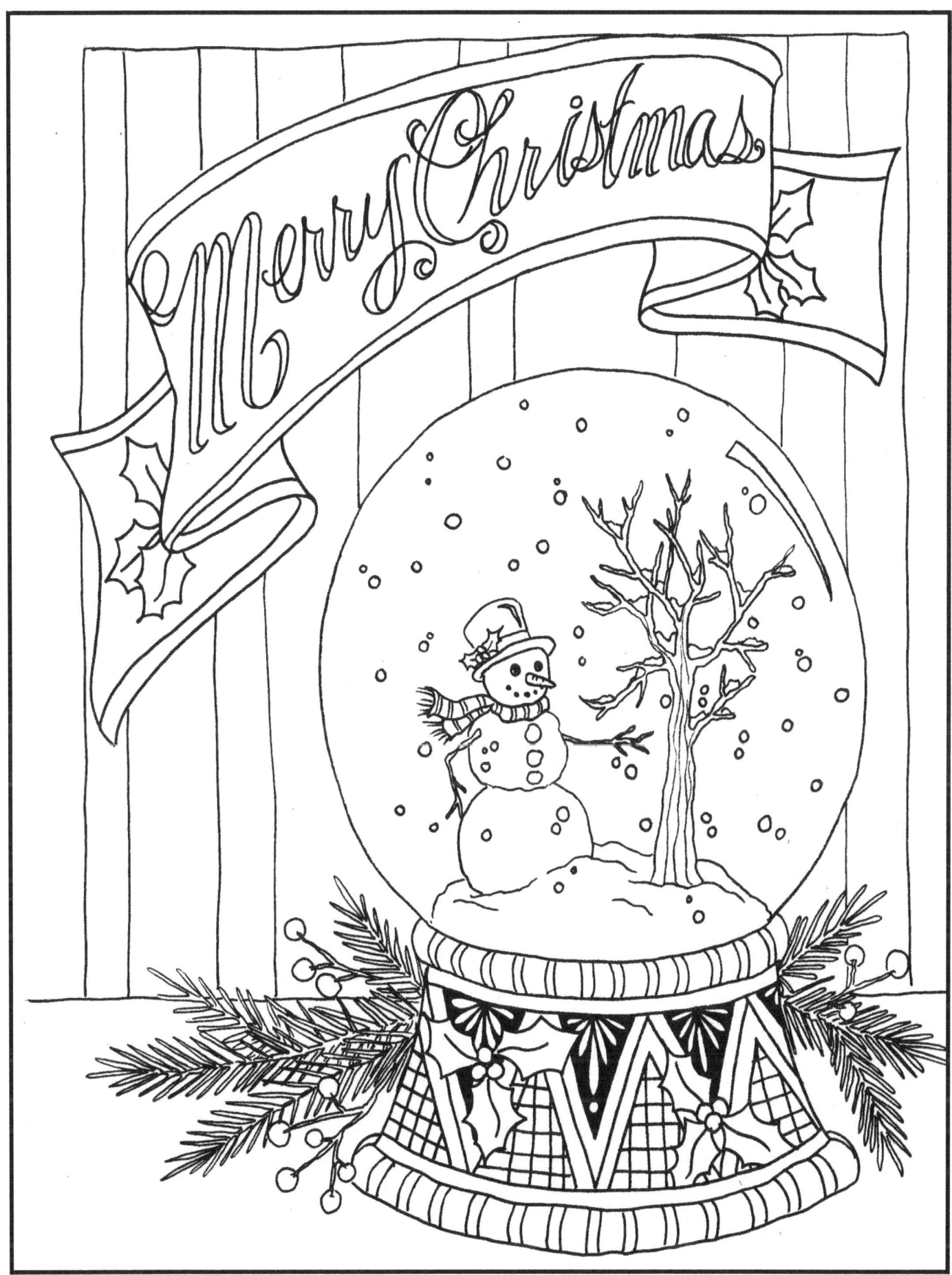

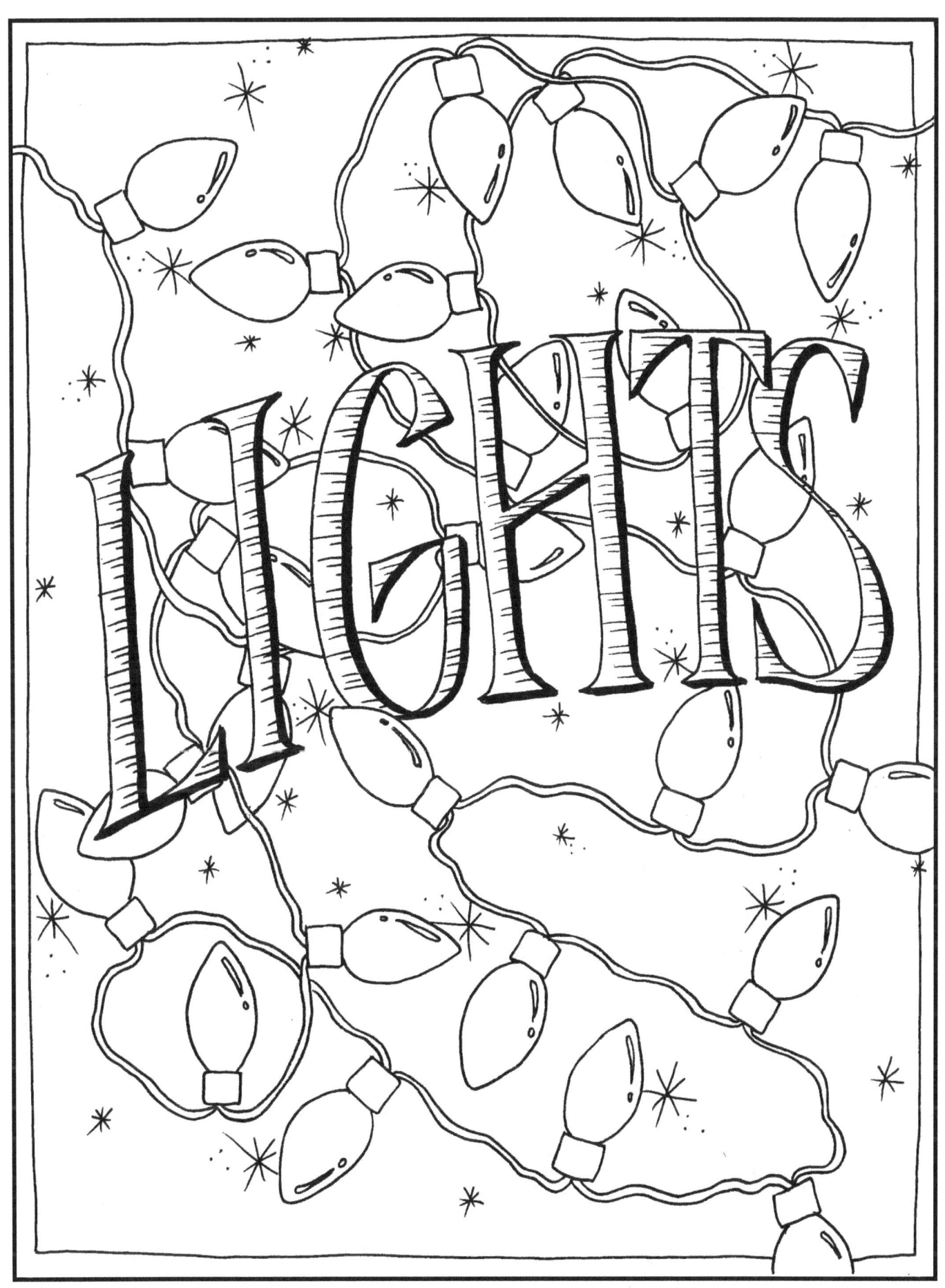

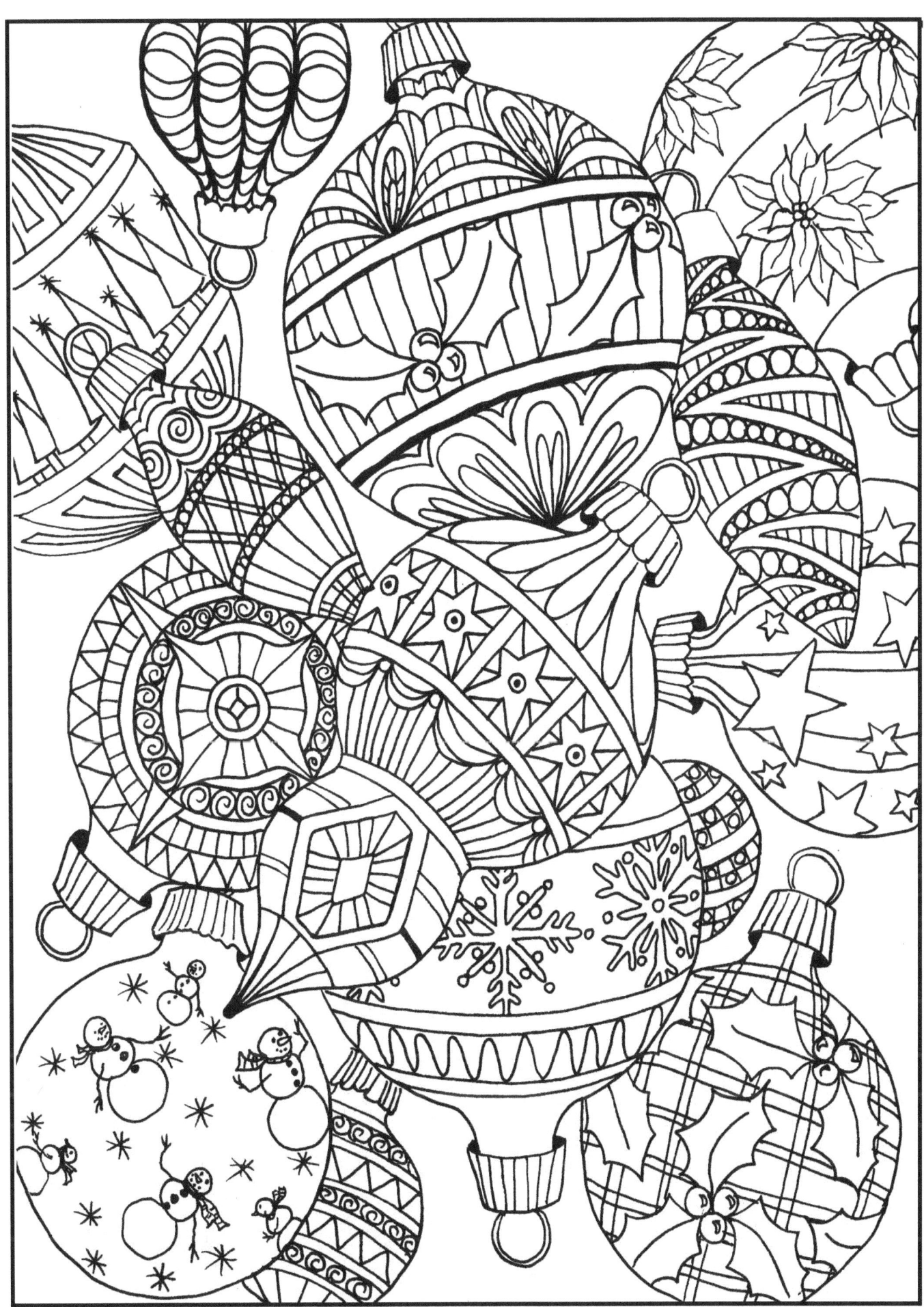

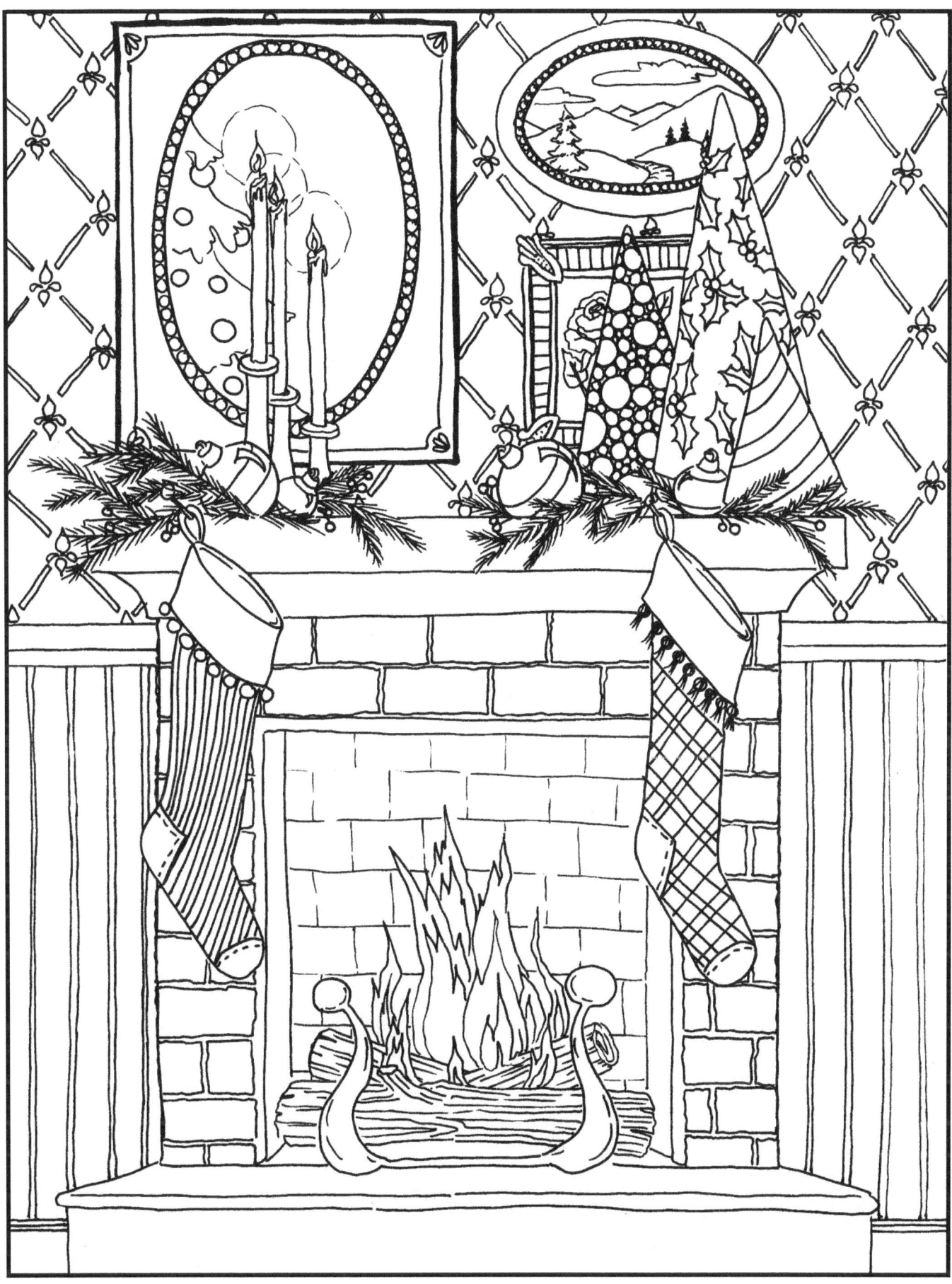

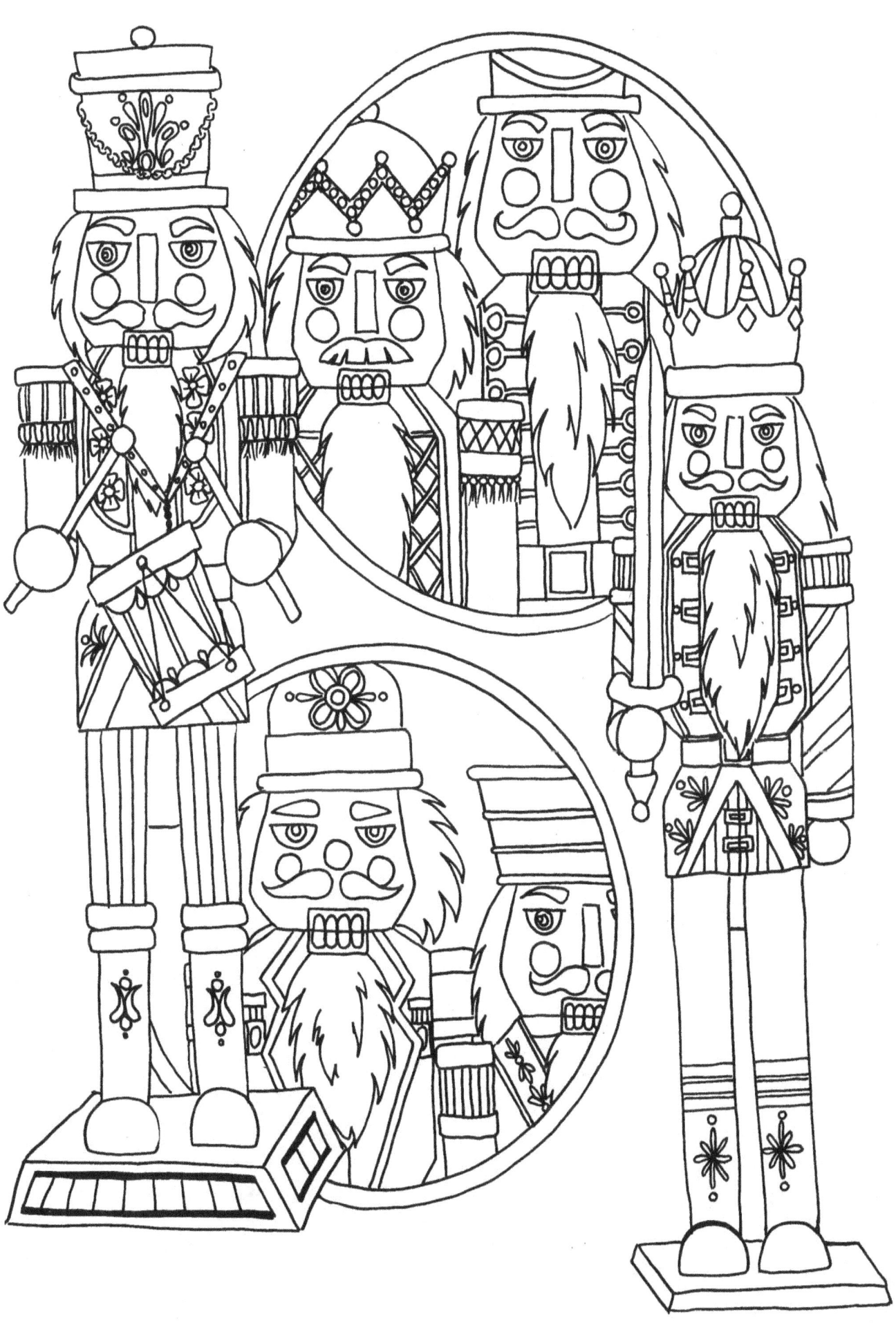

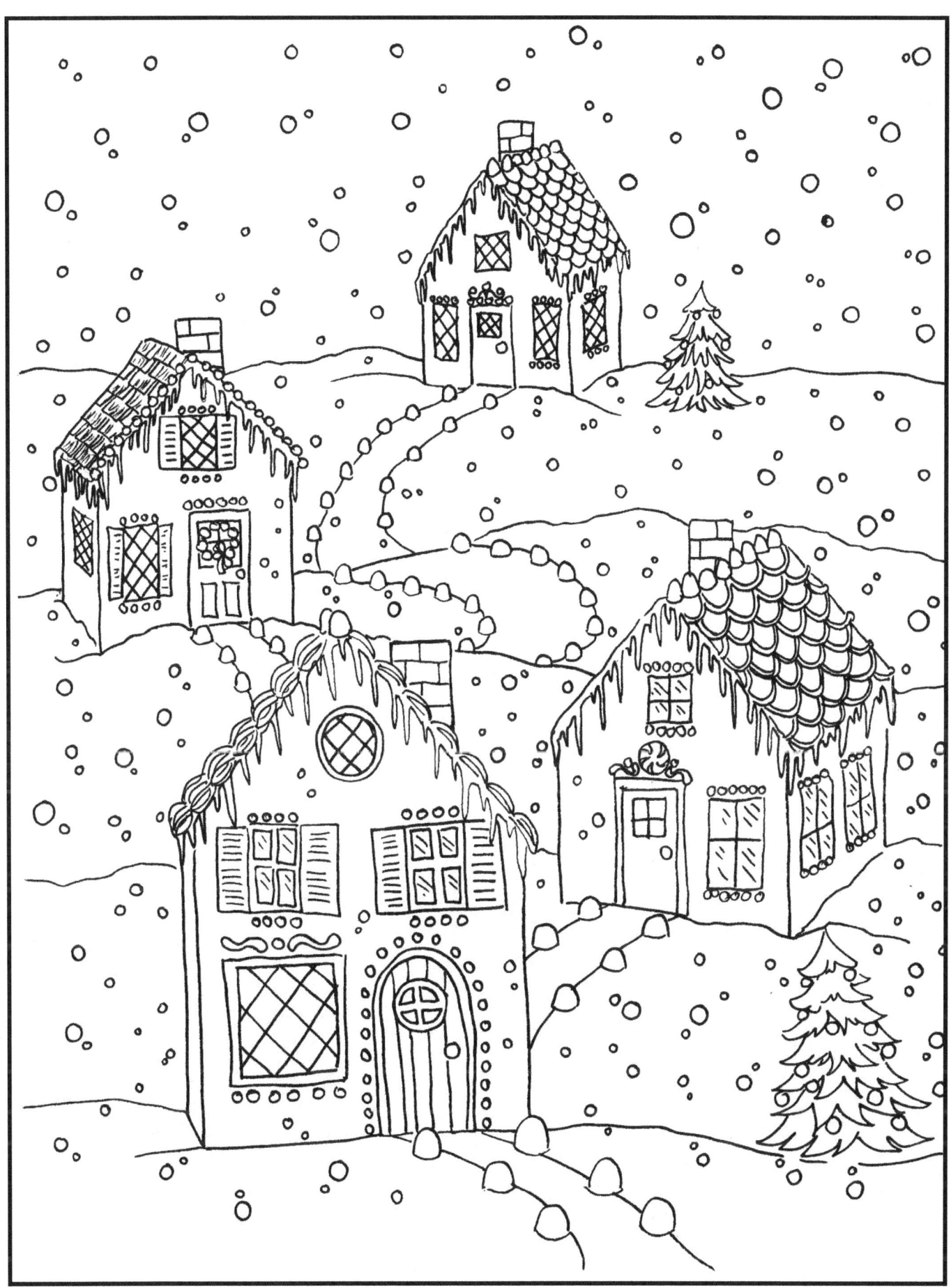

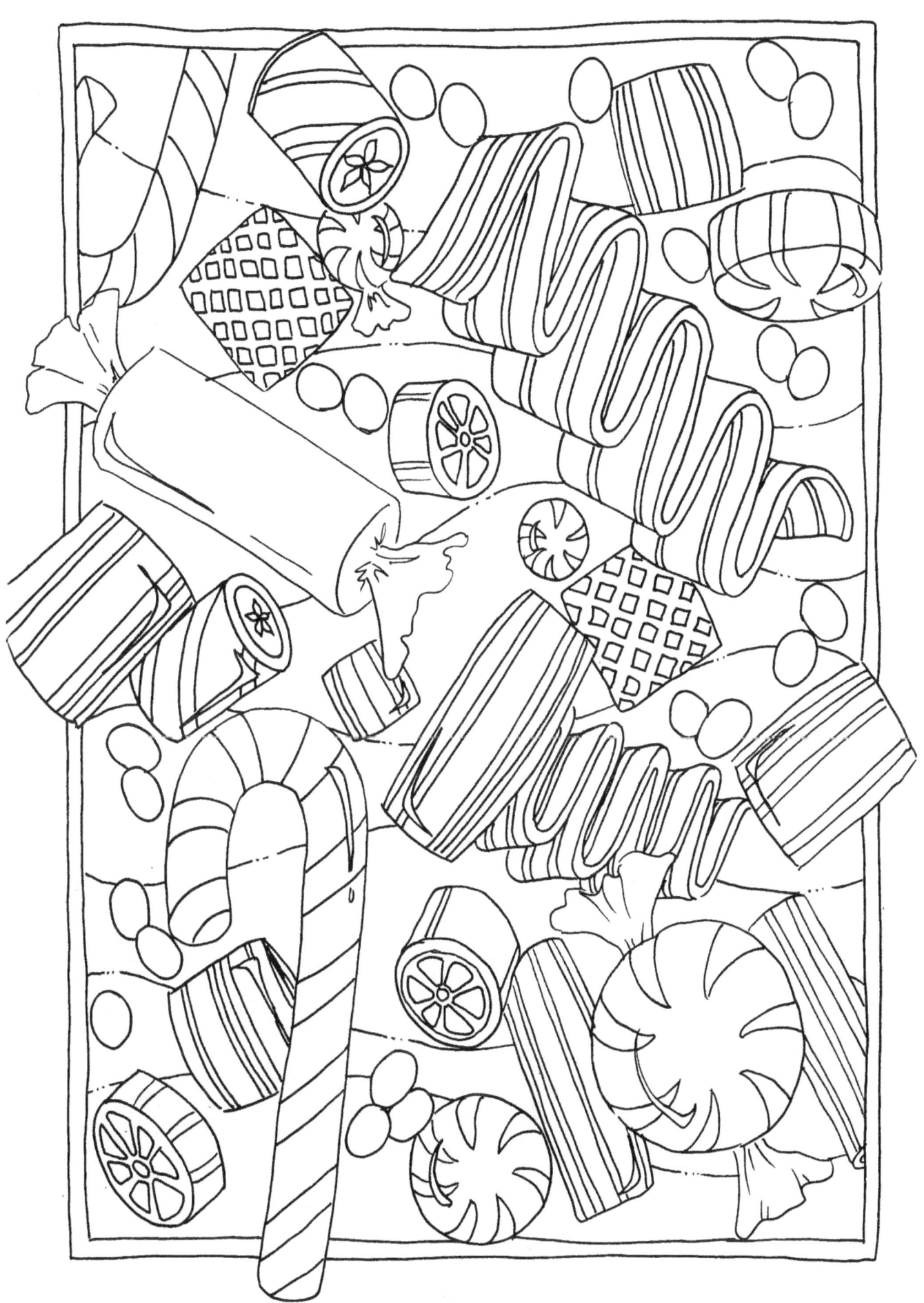

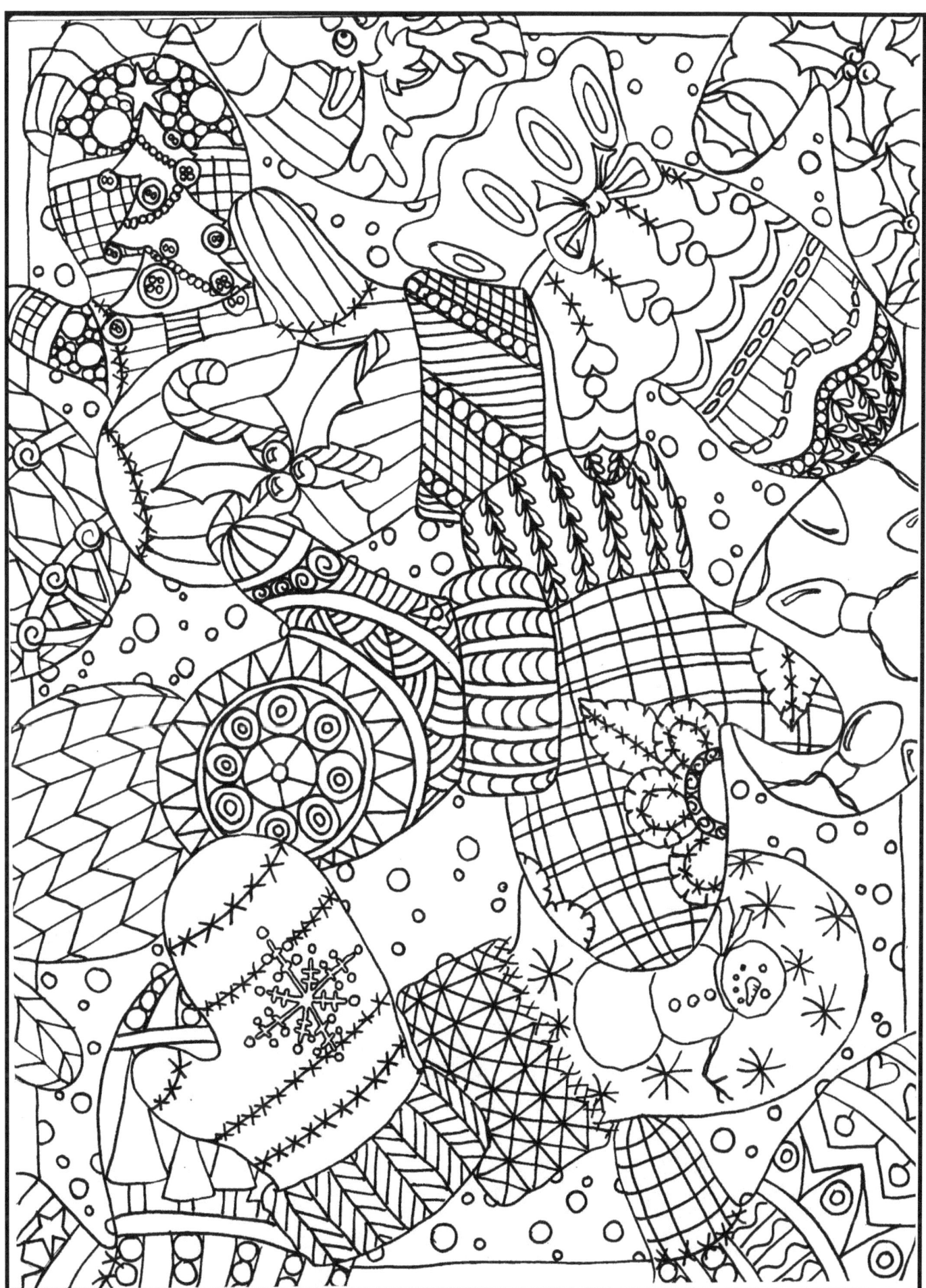

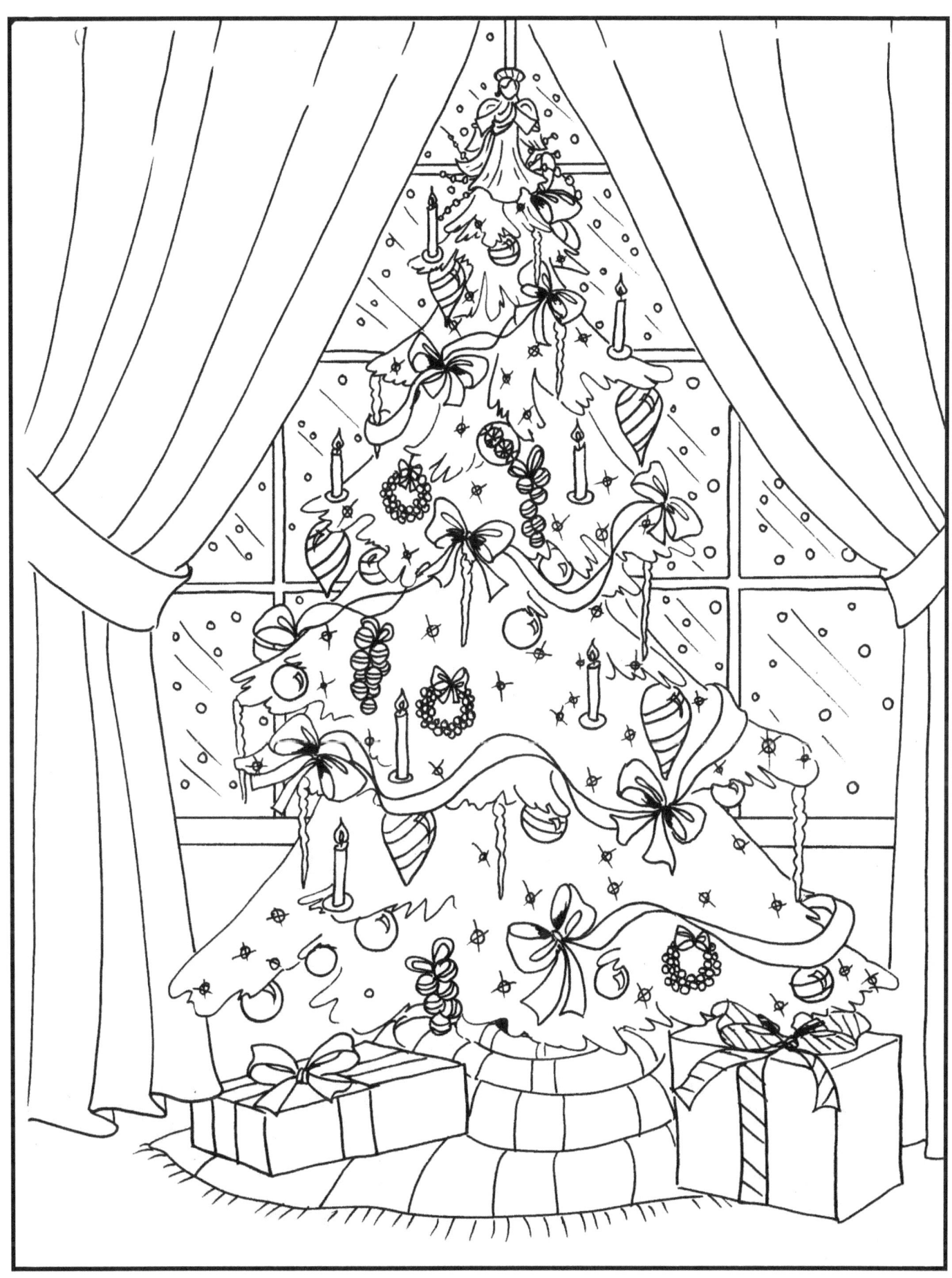

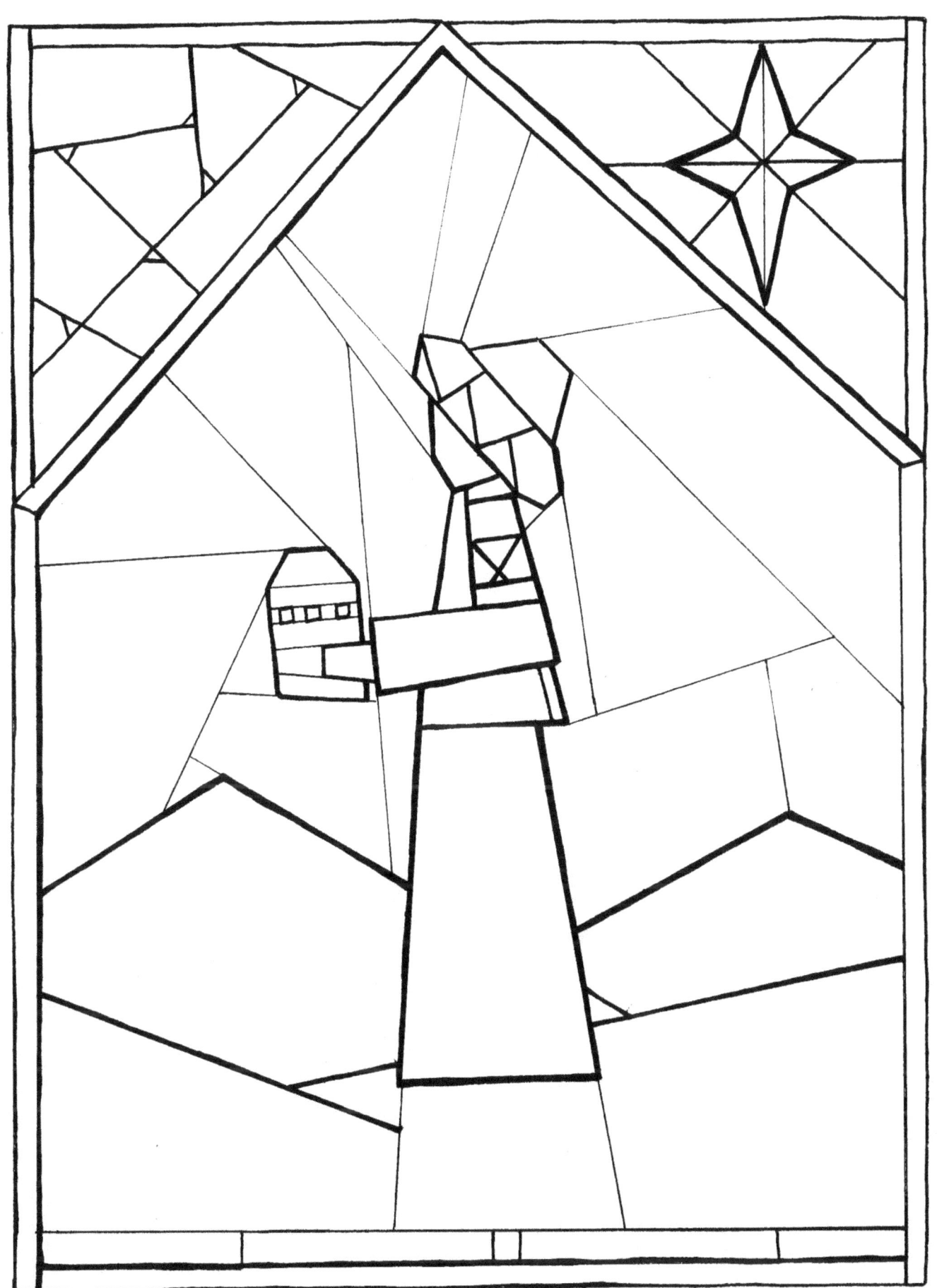

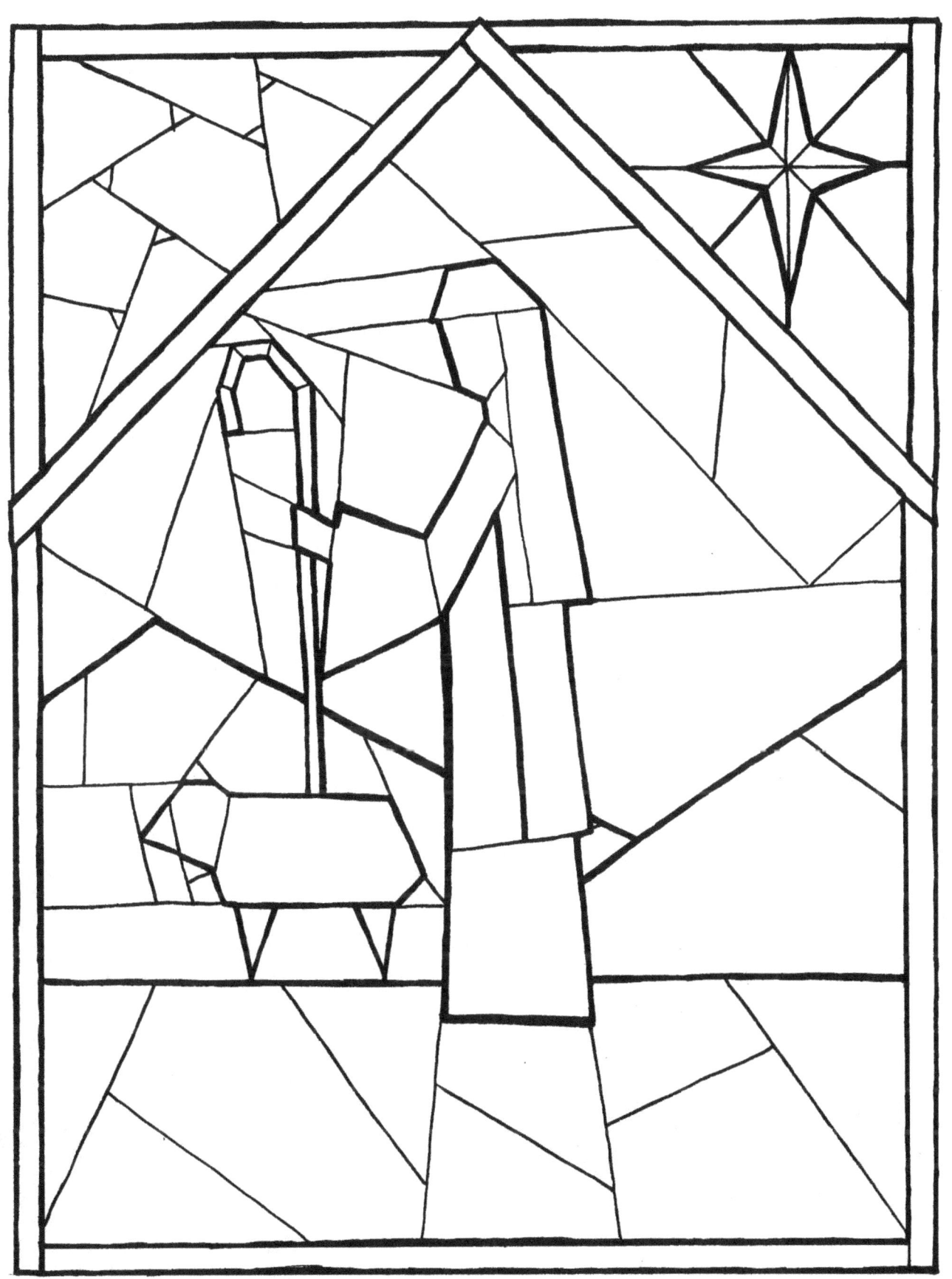

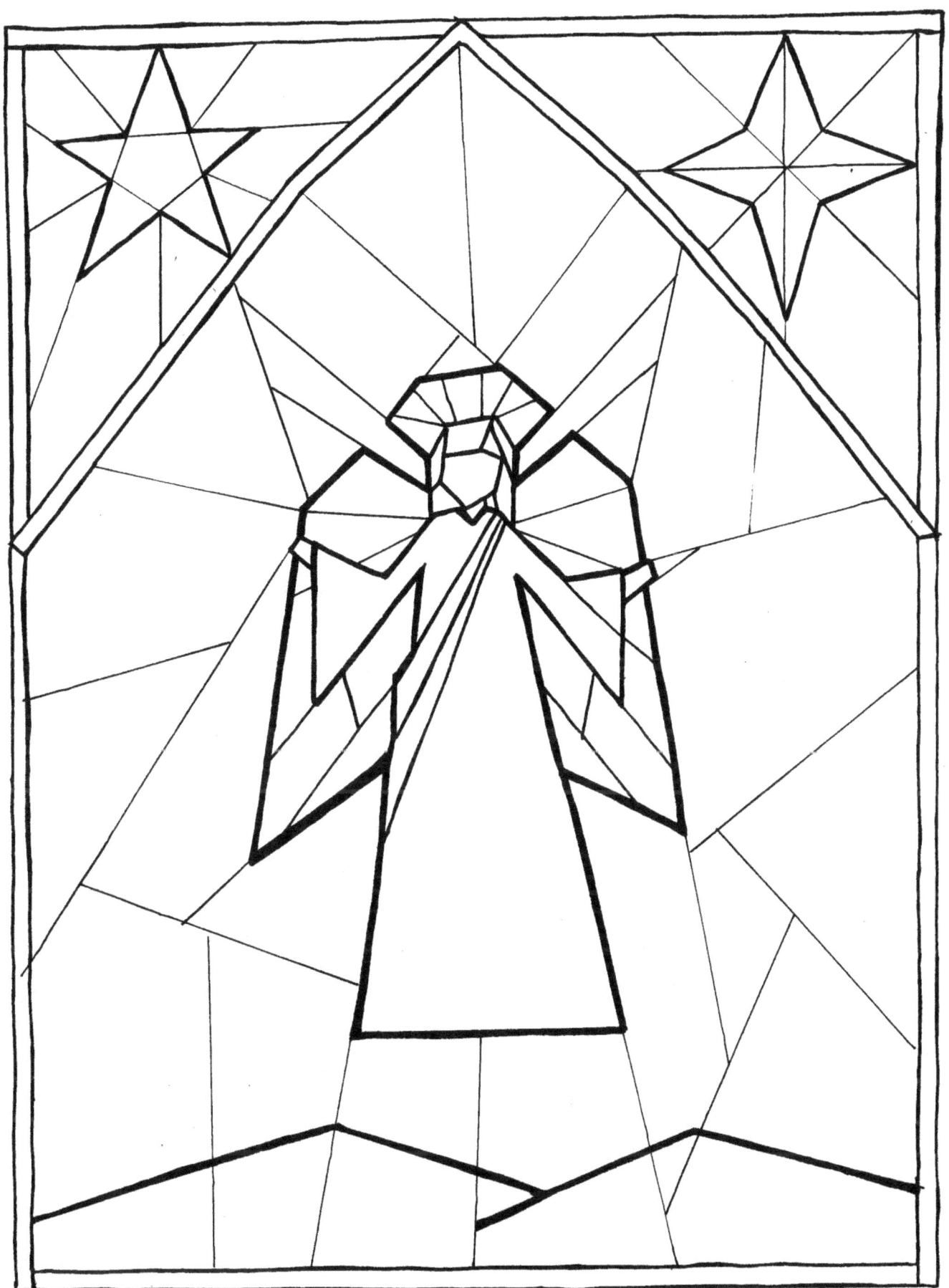

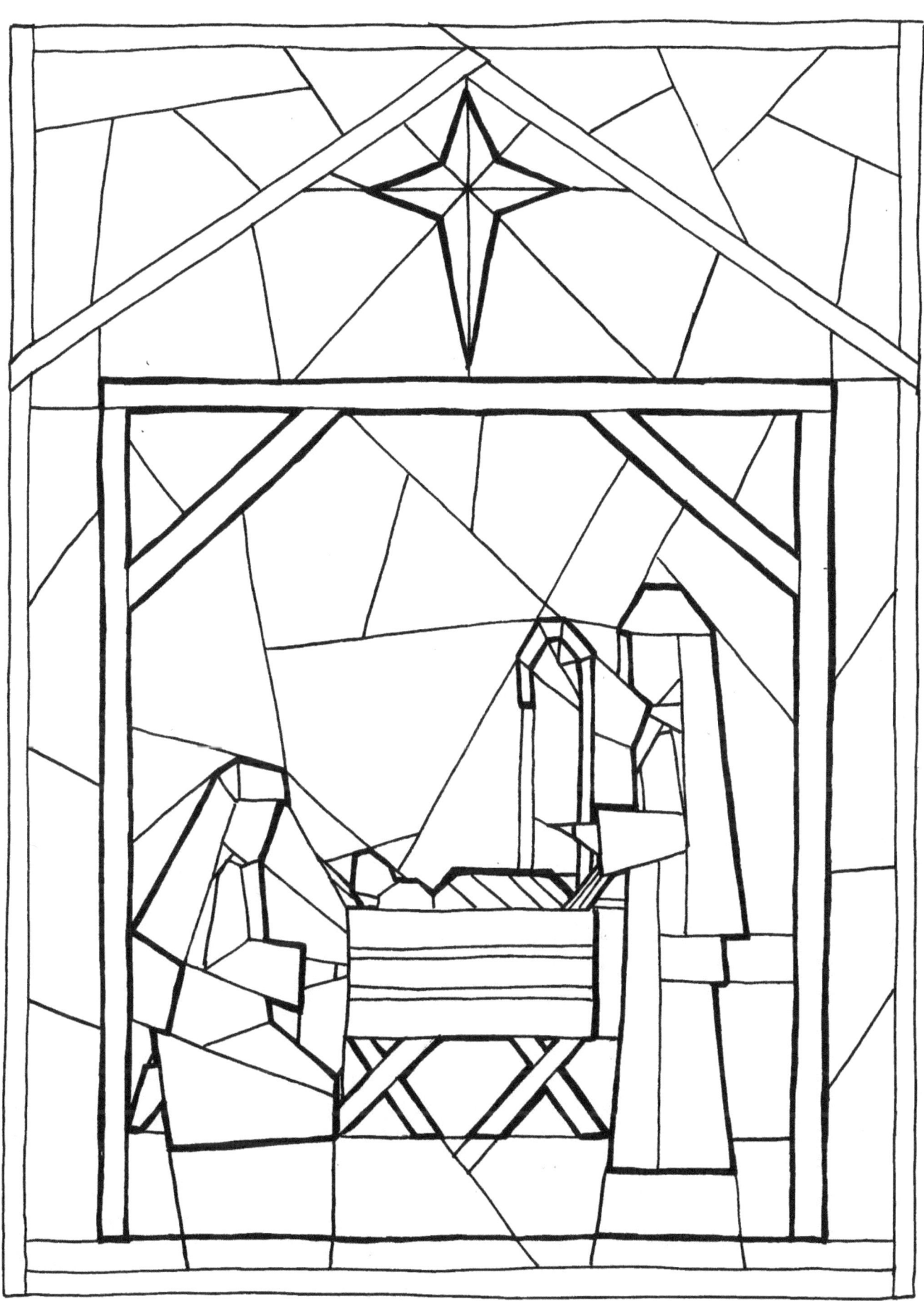

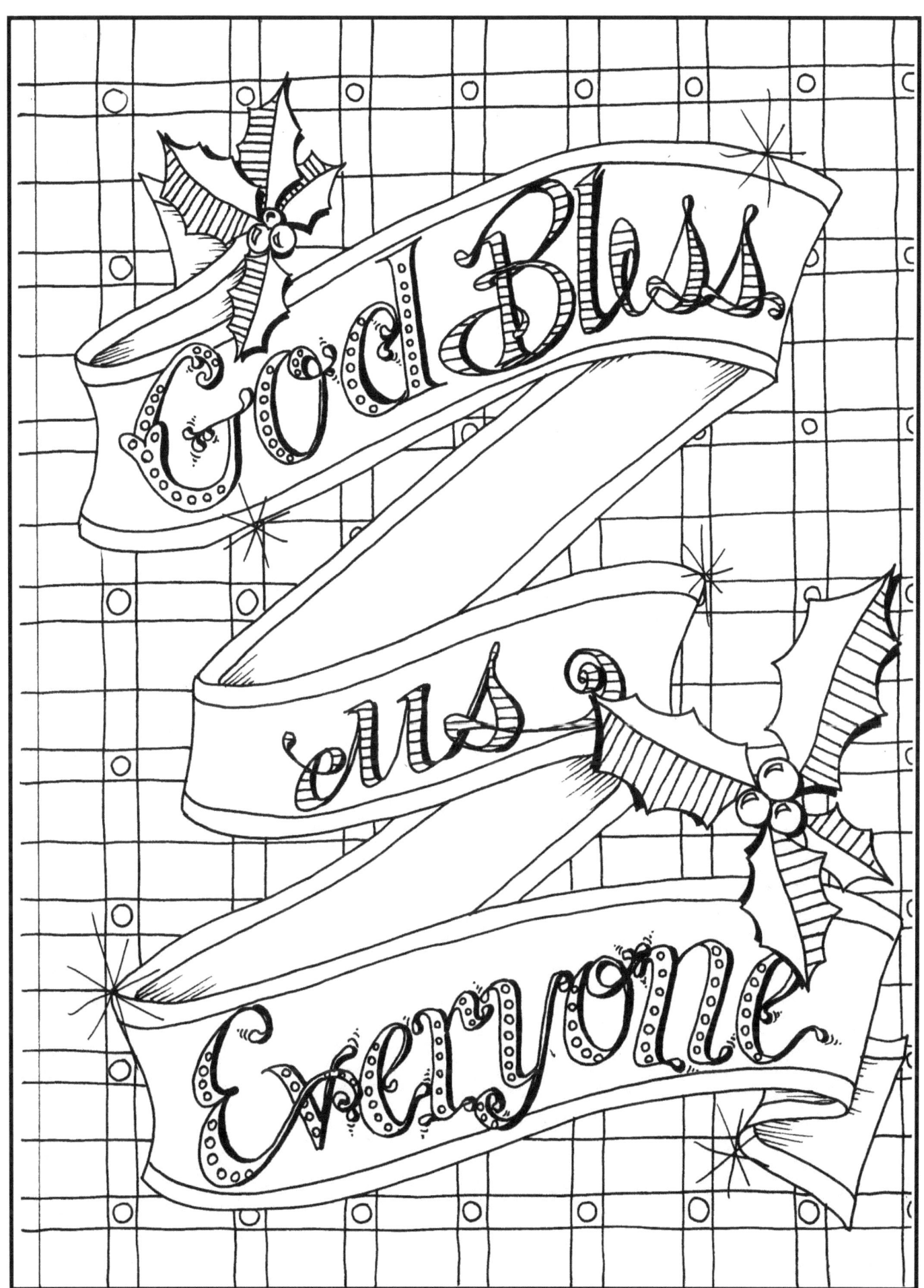

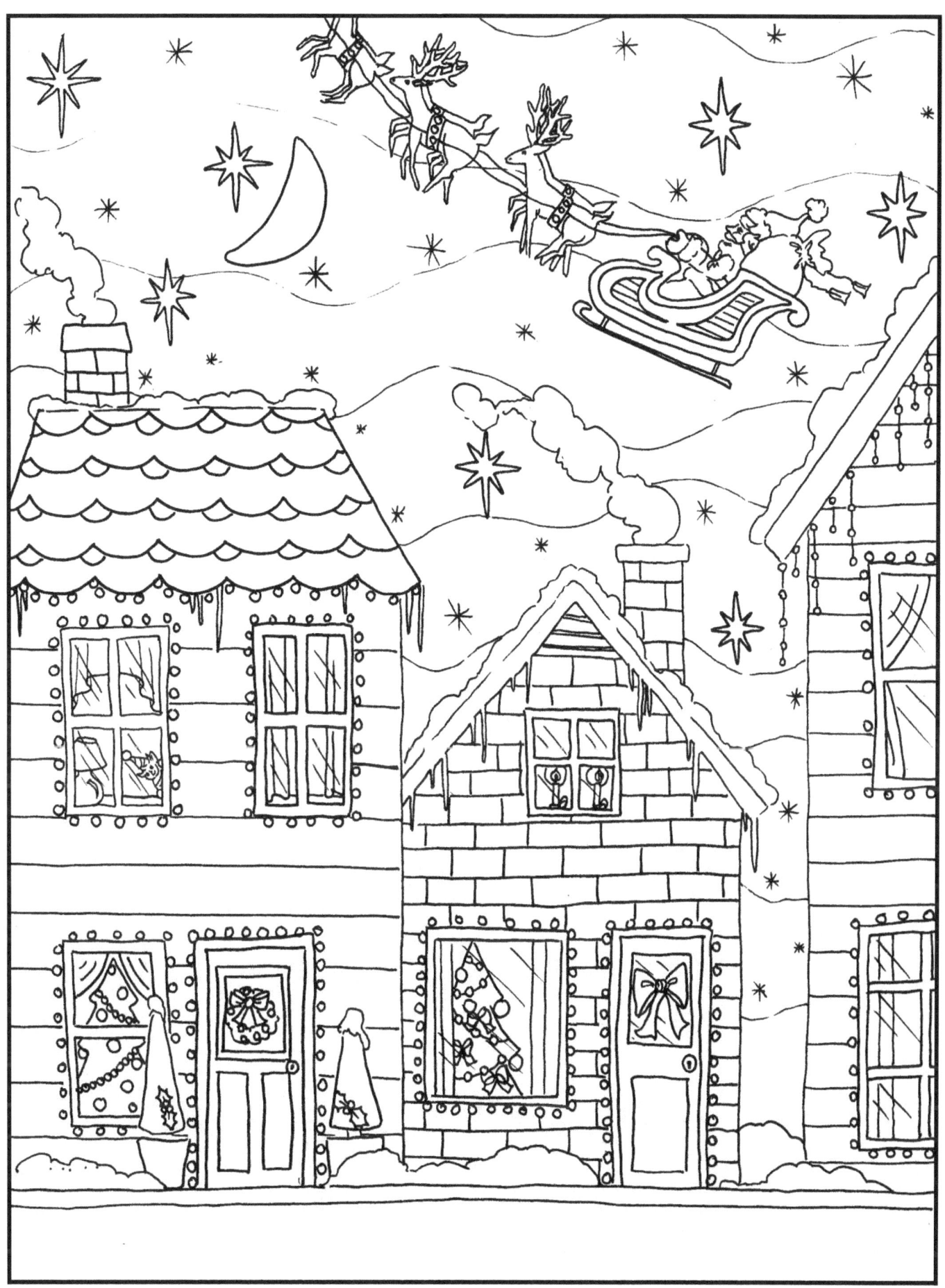

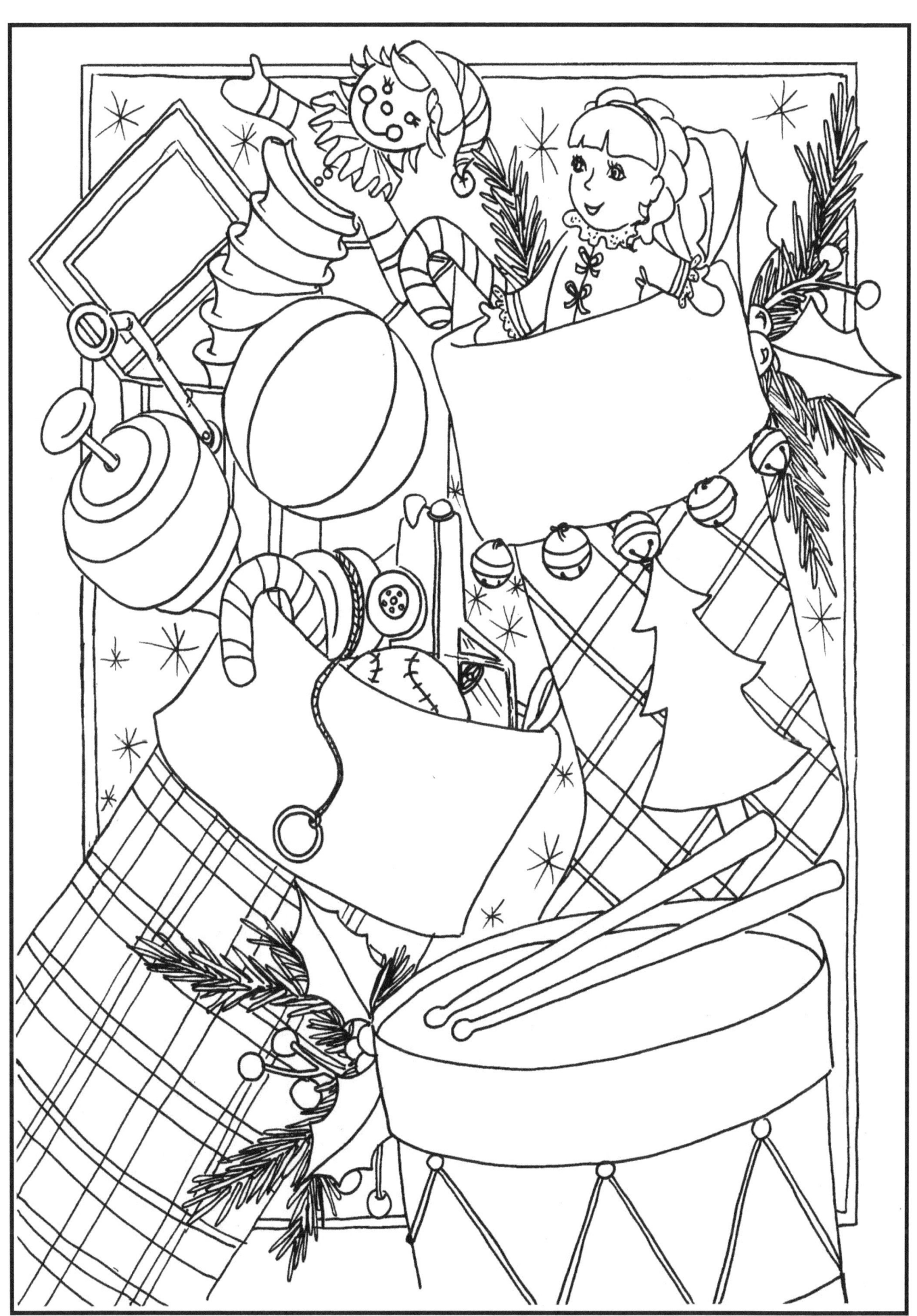

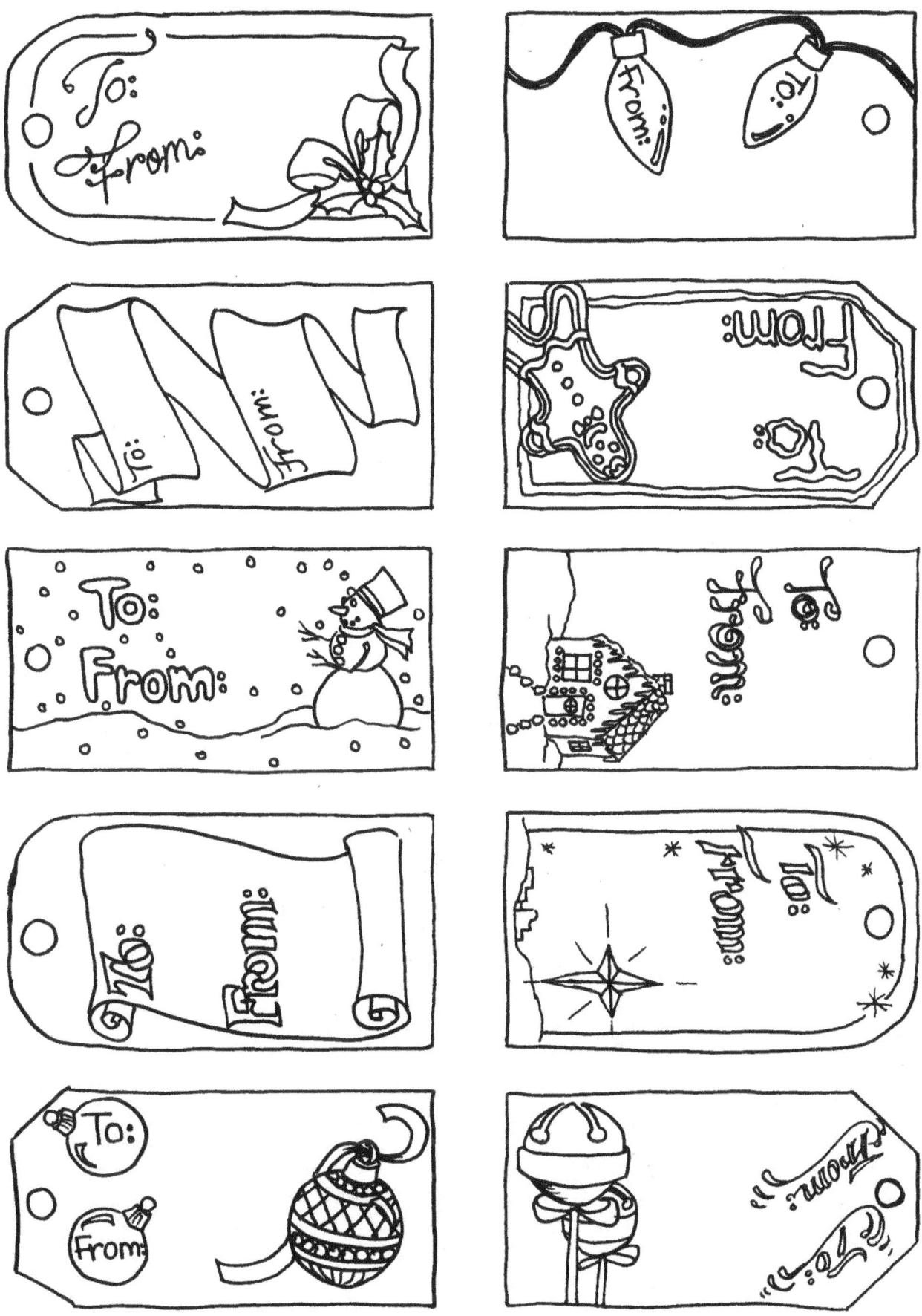

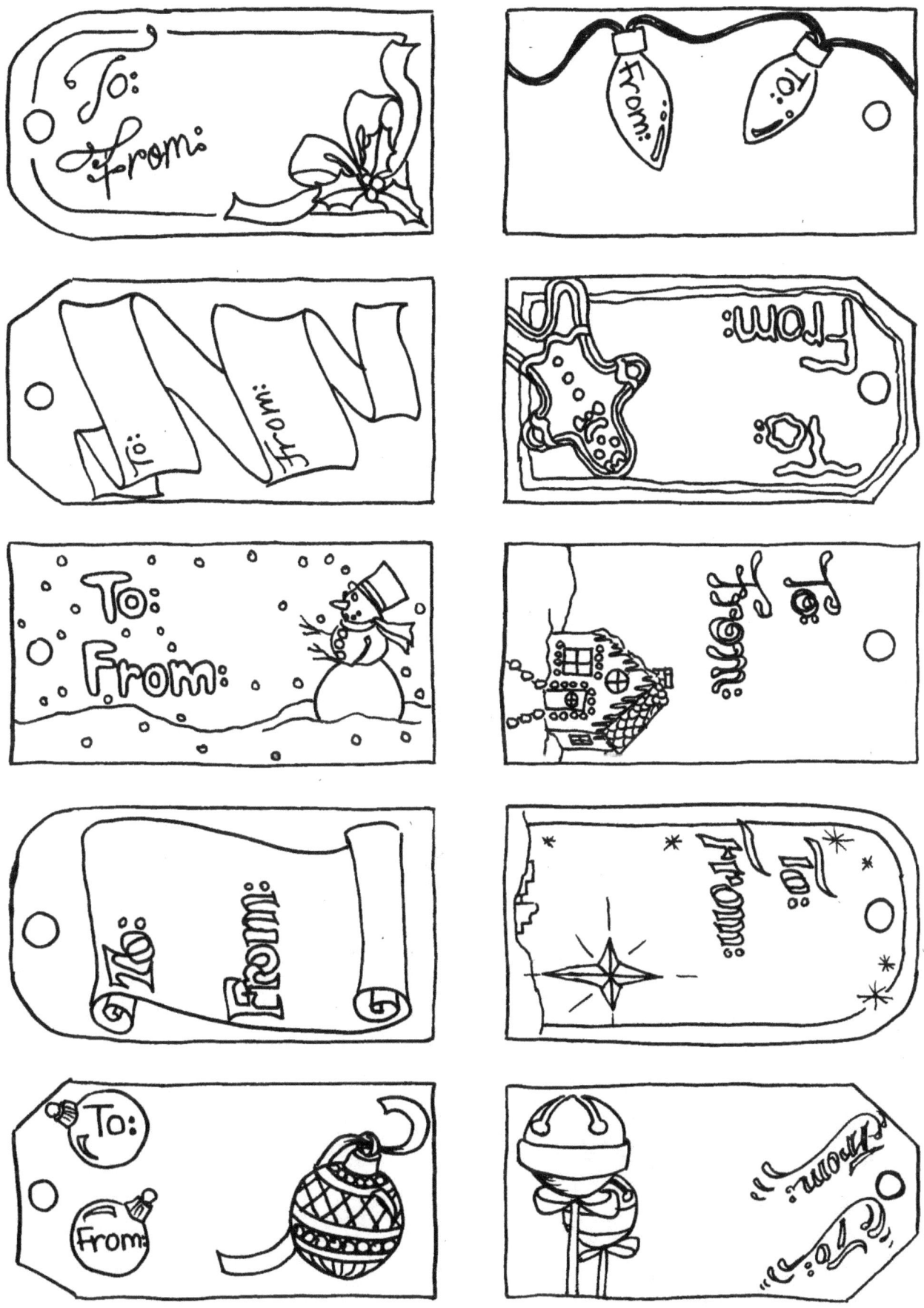

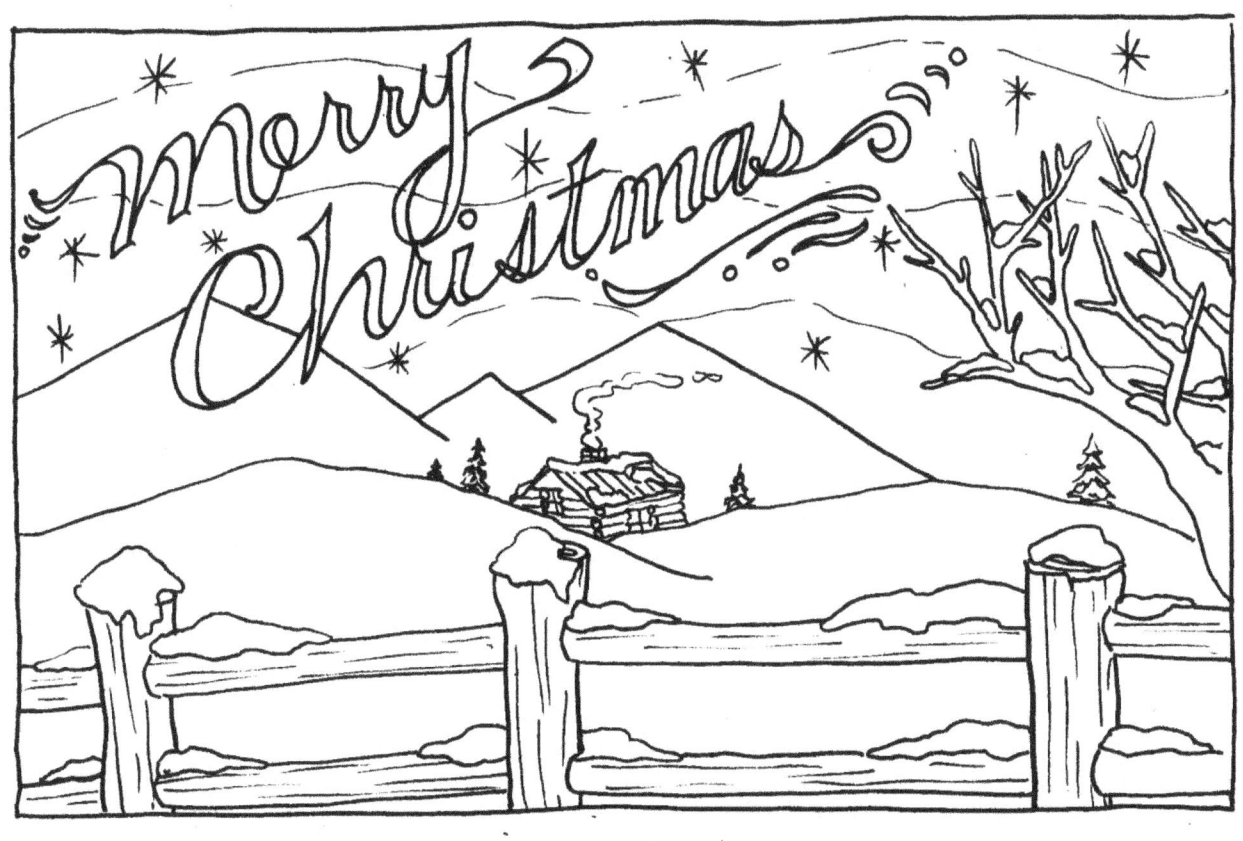

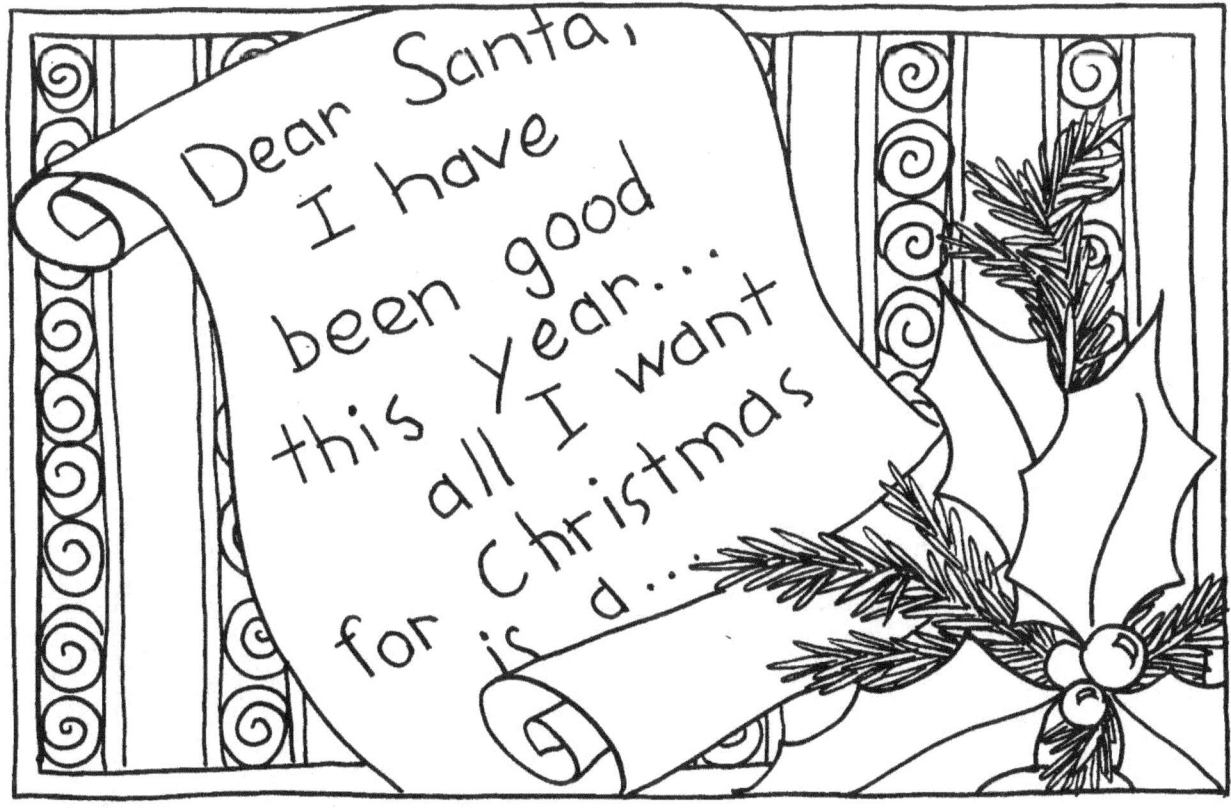

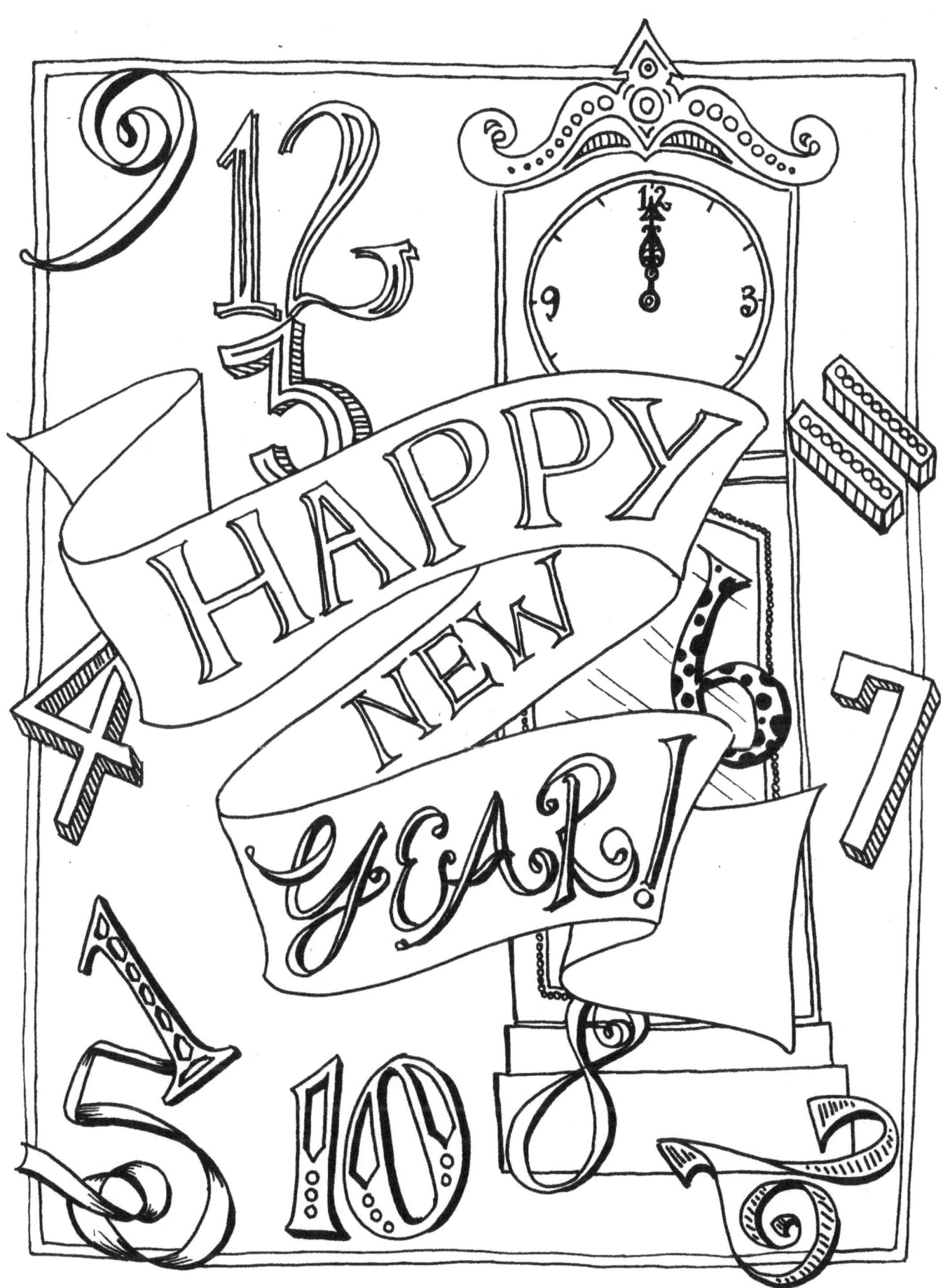

ABOUT THE AUTHOR

Gayla McDonald is an artist, teacher, and singer.   She lives with her family in a
small town in Montana.
She loves to be creative and enjoys making moments special for those around her.
She enjoys Christmas 24/7, 365.   It is her sincere hope that these drawings will
inspire the true Spirit of Christmas in all who bring color to these pages.